ANGELS WEEP
AND OTHER POEMS

Ian Hibburt

First published by Busybird Publishing 2020

Copyright © 2020 Ian Hibburt

ISBN 978-1-925949-99-5

This book is copyright. Apart from any fair dealing for the purposes of study, research, criticism, review, or as otherwise permitted under the Copyright Act, no part may be reproduced by any process without written permission. Enquiries should be made through the publisher.

This is a work of fiction. Any similarities between places and characters are a coincidence.

Cover image: Ian Hibburt

Cover design: Busybird Publishing

Layout and typesetting: Busybird Publishing

Busybird Publishing
2/118 Para Road
Montmorency, Victoria
Australia 3094
www.busybird.com.au

*I dedicate this book to all my special friends
And to Dianne, my soul-mate and inspiration.
Also the others who have helped.*

*Special thanks to Margaret, Ruth, Lynette and Pam,
for all their encouragement.*

Contents

CHAPTER 1
LOVE 1

CHAPTER 2
TRUTH & CHANGE 13

CHAPTER 3
GRIEF 31

CHAPTER 4
ETERNITY 45

CHAPTER 5
NATURE 57

CHAPTER 6
EAGLES 69

These poems have been waiting to be written for years. I have finally looked beyond my tears and fears and picked up my pen and started writing.

I hope these poems resonate with you and help you to connect to the larger universe out there just beyond our perception

Ian Hibburt

CHAPTER 1

LOVE

Angels Weep

Two honest people seeking true love
Wanting, wanting to belong
To another with love as strong.
When they have found each other
Loving without caring the cost.
My all, for you.
Your all, for me.
Together – for all eternity.
But when we love,
Each other's joy we seek.
And Angels weep
To see such love,
So pure and free.
Love so gentle
And so strong.
And Angels weep for joy
And sorrow.

(For sorrow that they cannot become human to experience love like this.)

Waiting for the Love

I waiting, waiting.
Waiting for the love to come.
I'm waiting, waiting for the sun
to shine again.

Waiting for love's return.
Waiting till my
Heart begins to burn.
Waiting for the love
to return.

One day the sun will shine.
One day my heart will burn.
One day my love
will return.

And when it does
Hallelujah!
What a day that
will be.

TRUE LOVE

Today I experienced true love.
She knew my every fear.
She kissed away my tear
She filled my empty heart
with her love.
She gave without counting
the cost, my God!
How beautiful she is
to me.
I am overflowing with
love – she is healing
me with love.
God this is so beautiful.
My heart will never
be the same.

Where Love is Born

She loves me with a pure love
– no holding back.
Abandoning herself into my arms.
I am filled with her love,
My love comes to life.
Returning all my love to her.

Together we travel,
To the place where love is born.
Skin to skin, heart to heart,
Spirit into spirit, together one –
Her touch of love,
Heals my heart and soul.
Makes my body whole.
She is my angel of love.
Forever in love.

Fly My Angel

Find your wings my angel
And with me fly.
Not into the past,
Still full of regret.
But into a new reality,
That we haven't experienced yet.

Beyond the barriers
Behind which we hide,
lie undiscovered lands.
Cut loose and trust your wings.

Fuel your dreams with joy and hope.
The great wide open is out there -----
Let's go.

Missing You

Oh love of mine I'm missing you already.
My heart is so full from loving you.
You fill me and make me complete.

To love you to the end of time
Will be a pleasure divine.
I'm missing you my love of mine.

I go to work but think of you.
I go home and think of you.
Counting the days, the hours, the minutes,
Till we are together again.

So deep, so deep.
Deeply in love with you.

ANGEL

Heaven must be missing an angel –
Because you are here.

Heaven must be missing an angel
Because you have come to earth below.
Just because you love me so,
To come to live with me on earth below.

You bring your love, so sweet,
You make my life complete.

Heaven must be missing an angel –
Because you are here.

Every Inch of You

I love you, every inch of your perfect body.
Today I experienced the joy of loving you.
And together we walked the path of love.
To that secret place where all our dreams
Come true – laying here with you.

All my empty places are full with your love.
I am complete with you.
We are love.

This may never end!
The joy of loving you.
My dreams come true.
Every part of me is now part of you.
We are together forever.
Flying into eternity above.

THE RIVER

Down by the river they wandered
To their own secret place,
The water sang its song
Over the rocks and sand.
The glade was full of flowers
And light, birds in flight.

And they performed that act of love,
As old as all time.
They joined in love so pure and free.
The sky so deep and blue.
Trees so tall and flowers so sweet.

Such a day as this may never come again.

NEVER COME BACK

I am floating, floating –
is there no end to this beauty
I see.

Such beauty right next to me.
Loving each other
So close, so warm and free.
Such ecstasy our bodies
Move as one –
Bliss and Joy is pulsing through our veins,
Till only our love remains.

Pure and clear shining over us.
We are complete.
We have followed love to its far horizon
And then gone on forever.

We will never come back from this.

CHAPTER 2

TRUTH & CHANGE

THE WORLD HAS CHANGED

The world has changed.
Or is it me that's changed?

The thing of beauty I never saw,
The sparkle of sun upon the flowers.
The hope and love I could not see.
My world to me was dark and sad.

One day an angel said to me.
"Open your eyes and see what you can see.
It's always been there just waiting for you.
To see with eyes of love."
Blessed from God above.

So I opened my eyes
And began to see.
So much beauty and joy in this world.

The world has changed
Because – I have changed.

INTO THE DANGER ZONE (AGAIN)

I used to live in a castle safe
From the world and any enemies.

But, in reality I was
A prisoner to my fears.

Time to let down the drawbridge
And walk out into the world.

I don't need a castle.
I have my own strength and protection.
Use it and God will reward my faith.

ANGRY/SAD

I get so angry and so sad.
When people treat me so bad.

Angry that they do not know me
And hate me for being free.

Sad because they are missing out,
On the real thing here.
Sad that they could all walk
Out of their cages and be free.
Just like me.

Why don't they?

Happy/Sad

Sometimes you must experience the sadness
Before you can enjoy the happiness.

I was taught to control,
Even deny, my emotions.

But that is stupid –
Why go through your life being careful.
Some of your laughter but not letting go.
Some of your love but not all of it.
That's not living!

Give me all of the emotion full on –
Let me love till my heart is about to explode.
Let me grieve like it will never end.

Let them go –
Let emotion colour your life
With its full technicolour spectrum.

It won't kill you –
It might even make you into someone
You would like to know.

So I will shed tear of joy or sadness
But, life will not pass by without
Me feeling its highs and lows.

The Flow of Life

It's a strange thing.
But when you are in the flow of life
It's energy lifts you and takes you
Where you want to go.

Don't fight it or react,
But fly like an eagle
On the winds of eternity.

I would normally be stressed, anxious
But, doubts and fears dissolve and disappear.
And I am flying.
Smashing it.
Making it happen.
This is sweet, this is smooth, this is being.
In the flow.

Complete – Not Old

The round worn boulder on the beach –
Smoothed by tides of time.
Complete in shape and design.

We have been worn to our shape,
By the sands of time
To our own shape by design.

Distilled and refined
The best of our life
Now clearly defined.

No longer youth's reckless drive.
No longer wild desire to be alive.
The game is reaching its end.
We are ready, eternity to spend.

THE TRUTH

Sometimes the truth is hard to bear.
I say to myself,
"I don't care!"
But the cold hard truth is always there.

Those difficult things that hold such emotion.
In the facts
I prefer to deny.
I would rather fly away and be free…

Why is it some truth is easier to deny
Than face the awkward facts that go against our cherished beliefs.
Whatever we do, we want to dream,
That it's true.

But the cold hard light of day
Destroys the dreams of Xanadu
Cold light of day showing the way.

I know it's not all bad.
I know I've had many victories and wins.
Why do I still deny those little truths
That show my defeats.

I don't want to know the truth
That will shatter the dream
Into a thousand pieces.

What's done is done.
I must face the facts.
Look them in the face
And admit my inevitable defeat.
Wishing won't make it go away.

We avoid to confront
The truth that we have failed –
That we have got it wrong.

It's the pain of knowing
That we failed that we avoid.
We cannot bear it,
So we deny it –
Bury it far from view.
Pretend it did not happen–

Unfortunately it's like a seed
And under the ground it will grow
Until it sprouts like thorns and thistles to torment us more.

What is the answer to this dilemma?
I could continue to deny the truth of my inevitable defeat –
Or face it bravely with faith and strength to heal.

I will let the hammer fall and crush my failed dreams
Upon the cold anvil of truth–
And allow my heart to heal –
To let it go.
Rip the thorn out of my heart.

I think I can do this.
"Love others and they will love you back."
But that is not true.
Your bank statement tells you that you have failed.
"It's worse than you thought."
Your dreams of success are smashed in the cold light of day.
I cannot make this go away.
What shall I do?

It's like this–
Some dreams were never going to come true–
But were there to keep your Hope alive.
To get you through the trials of life.
To see a better day when all this pain would go away.

They have served their purpose
And now I must let them go
With a grateful heart for the help they gave.
Time to take a breath,
See what's left.
What has survived.
Joy in my heart that I am still here.

I will not fear the truth
That I did not do as well as I intended to.
But hey, I was not to know
That some things I thought were true
Were never going to come true the way I wanted.

Oh God, it hurts to see the cherished belief
held up to the light and see what really is there–
No don't look away and say it is not so.
I've denied this for long enough.

Bad guys still win.
Good guys still loose
Karma is a fantasy for people who want revenge.
Promises of Heaven for us and Hell for them–
That's not helpful.
Keep working hard and you will succeed.
Well maybe.
And maybe not.
Do the right thing and you will be rewarded.

Just do the right thing
Because it is the right thing to do –
Without promise of reward.

Clinging blindingly to my
beliefs in the face of their untruth.

I've had enough of this –
All this ends here and now.
I'm not doing this anymore.

"All those shipwrecks of failed belief
That litter the beaches of my mind –
I'm cutting off all those false hopes that they can sail away."

I'll not feed the dreams that have failed –
I will be grateful for them then walkaway –
Let them die.

I'll not deny the real truth
That tells me these things are false
And I have been had – led astray again.
If you like to believe some fantasy of rules and
rewards in Heaven and
safety in numbers.

I'm letting this go.
I don't know what will
happen but no more
fantasies.

The Mountain

They told him not to do it.
They said he couldn't do it.
But then he did—
He went and did it against all odds.

This is what I must do he said.
I must climb into the sky above
to see what is there.
Hard and cruel was the climb
and many were the times he yearned
for the comfort and
security of the Village below
but onwards, upwards,
through the snow.

He was never seen again.
Did he die when he
reached his goal?
Or did he discover the
doorway to other worlds
and is there now
exploring the vast
wide open?

So move on we must.
Leave the comfort of
the known.
And adventure into
the danger zone.

Those who do step out
and face their fears
are rewarded with
wonder and joy.
Facing their fears
and living their
life to the full.

Try Again

Try again the Angel said:
Don't give up,
You've got this made.

Try again, try harder.
Give it another shot–
You have the skills.

Be brave, be strong.
Take them on
And win the prize.

You have not time for fear.
No time to doubt.
Do it! Do it again.

So I faced my fear.
And forgot my doubt
And let my mana* out.
The fight in me has returned.
Back to claim my share,
Of life in all its glory.

*A maori word for power

EDGE OF REALITY

Along the jagged edge of reality.
My life is blown into shreds.
By the storms of grief and death.
Until my thoughts and feelings cease
And in that silence, in that space…

From the chrysalis of pain and suffering.
My new self is reborn.
Cleansed of all the past and fear.
Now I want life in all its glory and terror.

CHAPTER 3

GRIEF

Well of Many Tears

Down the pathway of grief again.
To the well of many tears.

Here I face myself,
Reflected in its mirror.
Here there is no escape,
From the pain of losing you.

Deeply I feel the pain,
Crying, crying then letting go.
I must empty my heart,
Before it can be filled again.

With hope and joy.
Love and happiness.

This Cup

I must drink this cup,
    Of grief and pain.

Only when I drink it all,
    May I fill it again.

With joy and happiness–
Pleasures that will remain.

ALONE

You have gone but I am still here.
Your smile, your joy has gone.

You have gone,
On above to God's eternity.
To journey with the Angels,
To that place where you are fulfilled.
At peace, at rest.
Forever blessed–

I'm happy for you.
I really am–

But I am alone now.
And I miss you, so much.
My love.

FLOWERS MAKE ME SAD

Flowers were our joy and happiness.
Expectantly we watched,
Each bud turn into a flower.
Sharing the beauty of God's creation.

Now flowers just make me sad.
They make me sad because,
They remind me of the good times.

We had…
That will never come again.

18.12.18

Flowers

Flowers floating in God's river of love.
Flowers signs of our love floating away.
Our sad farewell floating to be with you.
We give our love.
We remember you.

All the wonderful things you do.
We remember the care you gave us.
We remember the joy of each day with you.
We remember you with the flowers.
Floating in God's river of love.

Bitter Sweet

And then it stopped, and you were gone.
What we had disappeared, into the dusty past.
And I am empty.

Tears have washed away the pain.
And I don't want to go there again.
Bittersweet memories.

Bitter that you have gone.
Sweet that we had such love for each other.
I remember you my darling.

Ambushed By Grief

I've got this – it's simple.
Let's do it…

But, hiding in those bits of paper and photos.
Are memories that awaken the grief,
Still sleeping in my soul.

And I'm ambushed by grief.
And my calm demeanour,
Is smashed with a thousand tears.

And it is done – come and gone.
I'm back together again.
But the scar still won't heal.

…Not yet.

For My Love

The blood red roses have dried into blackness–
A memory of our love.
And I will take these tokens of love.
To our secret place where we met.
That one last time.

The river's eternal journey to the sea–
Reminds me of how we travelled.
Together, for all those years.
What joy and happiness we shared.
A gift of love and you are gone.

I cannot cross that bridge to Eternity until it is my time.
Till then, My Love.

Rocky River Crossing

The sun has bleached all the colours
From the paddocks of wheat.
Even the sky has turned the palest blue.
Shadows crawl across the rocks and reeds.
Campaspe water is bubbling through the rocks.

And here I am again.
At Rocky River Crossing.
It is here I remember.
My love of my life.
My wife, for all those happy years.

And I still miss you Robyn.
Love that we shared.
And I remember us.
This still our special place, sweetheart.

Goodbye

The time has come,
For me to say goodbye.
And I am crying my love–
You are now above.

And I am here alone.
We have parted,
After all these years.
To end, in tears.

Tears of love and joy.
Tears of sadness and hurt.
Tears of loneliness.
Tears of thankfulness.

Thankful that I met you.
Thankful for all the love we knew.
Thankful for the children,
We are so blessed.
Thankful for our life,
Together.

The good times and the bad.
The happy and the sad.
We were together each day.
Living our love,
Together.

And through it all,
We walked the path.
Of true love.
Of happiness and giving.

And now that path must end.
You to above, to dwell in God's love.
And me left here behind,
Some other thing I must do.

I will never forget you.
I will always love you.
But I hate goodbyes.
I hate the pain of missing you

But I must have faith.
That when my life is through.
I will be there with you again.

Goodbye my love.
Til we meet again.
In God's eternity.

CHAPTER 4

ETERNITY

Eternity's Edge

Standing on eternity's edge.
Wind of God's love blowing on my face.
My spirit opens to the vast beauty of God's universe.

Huge trees of life spreading their branches.
Across the indigo skies.
Distilling the knowledge and wisdom of the universe.

Exquisite moon flowers drop their fragrances.
To envelope the senses in pleasure.
I am enthralled – bliss.

Eternity's edge.
Where one life ends,
And another begins.

Out There

I'm out there now—
Beyond the comfort zone.
Out there where, no rules apply.
Far from the control of Earth.
Out here in Eternity
Where miracles are normal.
And the impossible is unknown.
Out here in the wonder zone.

Until I'm Called

I've been to Eternity's edge.
And stared death in the face.
I do not fear you anymore.
And one day I will walk,
The pleasant lands of paradise.

But not now–
My work on Earth is not done.
And I must complete my destiny.

But until I am called.
I will dance along, Eternity's edge.
Skipping through the portals of light.
In love's glow, moving in the flow.
This is what I know.

Want A New Life?

Walk through the door,
Into the Kingdom of happiness and light.
But to enter— There is one thing you must do.
You must leave all your baggage at the door.
Stuff you cannot bring.

Anger, bitterness and hate—
You must leave them at the gate.
Guilt and shame and fear—
Don't bring them in here.
Judgement, criticism, depression—
Don't belong here either.

So just come as you are.
And receive the happiness,
Of God's love and light.
It is good and it is free.

Is This Real

What is real?
What do you feel?
What do you see?
What do you want to see?
Look and it is there!
Feel the joy it is there.
Now tell me what is real?

It is what you choose to feel.
It is what you chose to see.
Life is what you want it to be.

And if it is not…
Change the way you feel about it.
Don't like what you see–
Look away to the sky.
And focus on joy and hope.

And that's what you will see.
That's what is real.

The Angel Speaks

Suddenly I am aware.
That I am not alone.
He has come to speak.
To tell me about what I seek.

The Angel speaks,
But not in words.
They could not convey,
What he has to say.

Visions of space without end
Inspiring thoughts, feelings.
And power burning in my soul.
Energy to make me whole.
Healing, fullness, complete–

Mere words cannot,
Convey what my angel has to say.

Portal

One day I saw it.
A doorway, a portal into another world.
I turned the handle, the door cracked open.
I pulled it full open.

And there in front of me,
Was a magical world.
Of truth and goodness.

With no laws and rules.
To confine and contain,
This joyous life – freedom.

How can this be?
It exists right inside me.
An alternate reality?

And I am free to come and go.
Into this fair land.
But I must leave judgement,
Condemnation, hate and fear,
Outside the gate.

This is true, this is new for me—
As different as night and day.
Just being here changes me.

This portal into a new life.

Just For You

There is a world just over there.
Through that gate and down the path,
Of goodness and light.
Where all that is wrong is made right.
Darkness disappears in its sparkling light.
There is no night.
There is no pain.
There is no fear.
There is no sadness here.
In this place created just for you.

Me

Me ... drifting in the darkness of space ...
Time has no meaning, I have no face.
Memories flow out into space.
I am drifting, drifting silent, silent–
Empty.
Maybe I am dead.
Is death like this?
I thought it would be terrifying –
Sharp and painful.
I flow through the Eternity,
Of space and time.
I am nowhere yet
Everywhere.
My spirit is scattering
Amongst the stars to be reborn.
I have returned to God.

I May Never Return

Overwhelmed by the beauty of this place.
The delicate elegance of the flower.
The quality of light so clear and pure.

Impossible creatures live here–
At peace and harmony,
With this universe.

The very air heals my heart.
And my mind zings with clarity.

This is my special place,
Where everything is a miracle of joy.

Gone to play in other Worlds.
I may never return.

CHAPTER 5

NATURE

THE EGRET

She stands elegant and alone,
Staring into the depths.
Poised like a statue in the lake.
Patiently waiting for the fish to swim,
Within her reach.

There is a flash of movement,
Instant and deadly.
The fish within her beak,
Is caught and eaten.

She stands elegant and alone,
Staring into the depths.

DRAG**O**NFLY

A blur of light and he has gone.
Ah but there he is, hovering next to me.

Whizz he's gone again.
This time a hapless fly in his jaws.
Death on wings to little things.

I admire the dragonfly.
Such speed and grace–
He is then gone and back again.

Fly free and far my friend–

THE PINES

The pines on the ridge,
Are singing in the wind.

The eagles glide higher and higher,
Circling the sun.

The wild ox wanders through the bush,
Seeking the sweetest grass.

Deep in the river pools old trout sleep,
Dreaming of the spring.

Crickets are singing their love songs,
From under the thicket.

Such beauty.
Such harmony.

Goulburn River

Today I stopped
By the river.

Four white cockies,
Flying over.

The river rushing,
Out into thirsty plains.

Birds happily,
Doing their thing.

This is time out for me.
From the rush and stress.

After this I will return refreshed.
With a clear mind and peaceful heart.

Yellow

The leaves of the Birch,
Have turned cadmium yellow.
Reflecting the last gasp,
Of Autumn sun.

And now the stark,
Branches of winter–
The chill of sleep,
The rest of Winter.

When everything dies.
And then in time,
Is reborn in the Spring.

So it is in our lives.
Sometimes we must let things die.
Let things go.
So that they can be reborn.

Tiny Creatures

Half shadows floating on gossamer wings.
Travelling into the forest of light.
Emerald green filters through the verdant leaves.

Glimmering glow of the tiny creatures,
Playing in the dark.
The velvet night is alive,
With impossible creatures hidden from sight,
To all except the believers.

Innocence

Daylight filters quietly,
Down through the amber leaves.

The gentle rustle of a breeze,
Winding its way through the trees.
With tales to tell of where it's been.

The measured tink, tink.
Of water dripping onto the ground.
Earthy, wet growing smells,
Of the bush that surrounds me.

And a thrush singing in the distance.
Thin and sweet, pure notes of joy.
My senses full of the beauty of this place–
Earth spirits live here.

I touch the ancient gnarled bark of a very old tree.
He is singing his song deep and low–
Humming to himself,
Content to be one with the Earth–

And suddenly I am flooded with bliss,
And pure emerald energy.
Wow, how is it I missed all this?

Your senses need to be awakened,
To the beauty that surrounds us.
The mundane is transformed into wonderland.

We have forgotten what we felt,
And experienced as children.
When we believed in the impossible.

When we saw the fairies,
At the bottom of the garden.
And had joy and love and happiness.

Innocence, joy, love.
Connection to God above.
Children playing in God's garden.

Why did we have to grow up,
And forget all of this?
We need to return
To the age of innocence.

Knowledge

Like some half remembered story.
Heard in the palace of my mind.

Like a swan flying high,
He does not know where.

Like a tortoise singing in the swamp.
About far lands he does not know.

This knowledge it comes unbidden.
From I don't know where.

But when I seek it, it is there.
And who can deny,
The elegant truth it tells me?

THAT SPECIAL MEETING

"Meet us in the glade, where the Campaspe flows" they said.
And so I followed the path down beside the river.
Beneath the gums.

Silent anticipation, a shimmer in the light.
And quietly they appear.
One, two, then many.

Creatures of the light, from that other world.
So close, yet so far are here
Auras of peace, love and laughter.

And a man as old as time.
Approaches and we meet.
Hand shake and a knowing nod.

"You have been accepted, into the family, into the clan," he said.
"And I ordain you to be a healer like all these," he said.
Indicating the crowd now assembled upon the slope.
They all looked at me – with eyes of love and acceptance.

A sea of love engulfs me.
Healing hands gently cleanse and heal my very soul at every level.
Think, feel, act, the magic happens
All becomes one and it is done.

MY SPECIAL PLACE

The sound of rushing water fills the air.
Deep and clear beneath the falls.
Among the gums and reeds.
Sitting on the water-worn rocks,
I feel the peace of my special place.

And in the pool under the cliffs the Bunyip lives.
Guardian of the waters, silently he glides past.
Swirls in the water he looks me in the eye.
And with a flip of his fins he is gone.
The magic of my special place.

CHAPTER 6

EAGLES

Out of Sight

The eagle flies high into the cerulean sky.
Riding the winds so confidently, so easily.

He is one with the wind,
He is one with the sky.

Into the setting sun, in the firey glow.
How far will he go?

And he is gone, disappeared from sight.
Following the sun, out of sight.

THE EAGLE

The eagle spreads its wings,
Basking in the sun light.

Full of energy, bursting into flight.
Soaring upon the winds.
Rising, circling till he disappears out of sight.

But, he still sees you.

As an Eagle

I am free.
Free to fly away.
My eagle wings are strong again.
And I must feel the wind in my feathers.
Lifting me into the sky.

Today I must fly away.
Leaving this prison—
Of my mind confined.
Keeping my thoughts,

Freedom cannot be bought or sold.
I must be won like gold
And many there are who would take it from you.
Evil ones with bad intentions
Knowing what is "good for you."

Now I'm free to fly.
And I am flying now.
Up beyond the Earth below.
Upward into the sun I go–
Riding the winds of God's love.
Into the sky above.

How wonderful to be free.
Joy in my heart.
Power of my wings.
Watching the world below.
I can see everything.
I am king of the skies.
And I am free.

Out of Here

I'm out of her.
Out of the security of living,
Behind the rules–

I'm leaving all that behind.
Chucking out the rule book.
That had my mind confined.

I am free to fly into the sky.
The cage is empty.
And I am gone.

The Moment of Truth

The young eagle is testing his wings in the wind.
His wings are strong and he wants to fly.
He sees the other eagles flying out there.
That's where he wants to be.

The moment of truth is here…
He must jump and fly.
A moment's hesitation.
And then he does it.

He flies – strong and free up in the sky.
Where he should be.
The young eagle is me.
And my moment of truth is here.

FREE TO FLY

There was a little Eagle who,
Became separated from its real family.
Who lived in the mountains.

The little Eagle lived with a kindly family,
Who fed and cared for it.
But they did not know,
About Eagles and what they do–

So they treated the Eagle like a chook,
And put a rope around its foot.
No you cannot fly!
It is dangerous!
Stay safe here on the ground.

One day a man was travelling in the area.
And heard about the tame Eagle who could not fly.
He bought the Eagle and took her home.
And fed her meat and cut off her rope.
Gave her hope–

There's the sky, that's where you belong.
Now that you are strong you are free.
To fly up into the sky.
And you can be wild and free.
Graceful and strong up in the sky.
That's where you belong.

And with that she flapped her wings,
And rose into the air.
Hesitant and careful,
Then with free abandon.
The joy of flying.

Be wild, be free.
The winds your friends.
The sun your guide.
And when I see her fly
Joy fills my heart.
Knowing that she is free.

Eagles are Flying

Eagles are flying high in the sky.
They are so high I cannot see them anymore.
But I know that they can see me.

High above invisible to me –
Like God I cannot see him,
But I sure can feel his love.

Oh that I could fly like an eagle.
Into the sky of God's love.

Owls and Eagles

I saw an eagle flying,
Hanging in the sky.
Watching, watching.

I felt an owl in the night.
Flying silently.
Watching, watching.

The Keeps of the secrets,
That we must know.
And we can ask them,
To share their wisdom.

One the guardian of the day.
One the guardian of the night.
Owl and Eagle,
Birds of might and power.

WINDS OF GOD

Like the eagle you must cut lose.
And abandon yourself to the winds of God.
Fly high and far.

Be free.
Experience God's great love
And wonder at his creation.
Fly high and far.

And when the time is right.
You will return…

Wings are for Flying

We eagles stand around all day.
Discussing the merits of this and that–
How interesting.
But no matter what you say.
There is no other way.
Face the wind.
Extend your wings.
And go – Fly.
Wings are for flying.
Become one with the air.
Grace and beauty in how you fly.
Master of the sky.
Just fly.

(After all you are an eagle.)